EP Sport Series

ep

EP PUBLISHING LIMITED
1976

epsport

basketball

Brian Coleman
Technical Director E.B.B.A.

Peter Ray
Coaching Officer E.B.B.A.

Acknowledgements

The authors would like to
acknowledge with thanks the
assistance of the following in the
preparation of this book:

Keith Stretten for his skill and
patience in photographing the
demonstrations and for the
photographs of our National Junior
Championship Final

Members of the Avenue Basketball
Club for taking part in the action
photographs

Picketts Lock Sports Centre for
providing the facilities for the
photographs

Speedo (Europe) Limited for help and
assistance with the photographs

Arthur Guinness Son & Co.
for the frontispiece photograph

ISBN 0 7158 0587 8

Published by EP Publishing Limited,
East Ardsley, Wakefield, West Yorkshire, 1976

Text set in 11/12 pt. Photon Univers, printed by photolithography,
and bound in Great Britain at The Pitman Press, Bath

CONTENTS

Foreword by K. K. Mitchell

Since 1949, when the English Basket Ball Association first set up a coaching scheme to train coaches and teachers of the game, many hundreds of coaches have been trained. Among the many coaches who have been through our training programme are the authors of this book. They both now play a leading part in the continued development of our training programme for coaches, teachers and players.

1 September 1965 was a notable date in the development of the Association's coaching scheme, when Brian Coleman took up his duties as our professional National Coach, with the brief of the technical development of the game of basketball. He came to the Association after a number of years teaching and coaching the game at all levels, having coached the Watford YMCA Royals to win our Junior National Championship. Since becoming our National Coach he has travelled throughout this country, taking training courses for coaches and players, and in Europe and the USA to further his knowledge of the game. The results gained from the coaching of all levels from national team players to beginners are to be found in this book.

Peter Ray, a contemporary of Brian Coleman at Loughborough College where they trained as Physical Education teachers, is now the Chairman of the Association's Coaching Sub-Committee. He has been involved in the production of wall charts and instructional loop films for the Association and has staffed many national training courses for coaches and teachers. From 1962 to 1970 he was coach to the England Schools Senior team.

The English Basket Ball Association welcomes this opportunity to co-operate with EP Publishing Limited to produce this well-illustrated book of instruction for basketball players. We acknowledge help received from Speedo (Europe) Ltd, suppliers of sportswear, in the production of this book, and offer our thanks to them and to the Avenue Club for their help and co-operation.

K. K. MITCHELL
Honorary General Secretary of the
English Basket Ball Association

Preface

In writing this book the authors have been conscious of the limited number of books that have been written for the basketball player. Most books on the game are written for the coach or teacher. This book aims to fill that gap and is written for the player who has been introduced to the sport and wishes to further his knowledge of this fascinating game—basketball.

Although the illustrations show men, the material covered in this book is equally suitable for women and girl players.

During the past decade we have seen a steady improvement in the standard of English basketball. One reason that has been advanced for this improvement is the greater understanding of the game gained by our leading players. It is the authors' contention that the improvement can only continue if this understanding of the game is gained by players involved at all levels of competition, from the beginner schoolboy to the international star.

Taking advantage of the well-illustrated EP Sport series, we have used the illustrations to show the basic techniques and skills of the game, and the text to highlight some of the details illustrated and to further the understanding of the game by the player. Even in a book as well-illustrated as this we have found space a limitation and we have therefore given only limited coverage to team-play, concerning ourselves with the principles of play and the basic individual and team skills, believing it is the responsibility of the player's team coach to select the most appropriate team tactic for the team to use.

This book aims to give instruction, to suggest questions the player should ask of his own play, and to help the player make the appropriate responses to the ever-changing situation in the game. It is our hope that the book will have a value as a 'coach yourself' manual for the player. The book assumes that the player has already been introduced to the game and is aware of the rules.

The basic individual and team skills covered in this book form the basis for every successful basketball team. For this reason, although the book is written with the basketball player in mind, teachers and coaches will find information and ideas on the fundamentals of the game that will help them in their own teaching and coaching. The game of basketball is continually developing and players, coaches and teachers at all levels should strive to increase their knowledge and understanding of the game. If our book achieves this in some small way with all our readers we will be amply rewarded.

For the benefit of players not conversant with the technical terms used in the game a glossary has been included at the end of the book.

Introduction to the Game

The game of basketball was invented by a Canadian Physical Education Lecturer, James Naismith, at the International YMCA Training College in Springfield, Massachusetts in 1891. Naismith used five basic principles in his new game; these were:

- there must be a ball which shall be large, light and played with the hands,
- there shall be no running with the ball,
- no man on either team shall be restricted from getting the ball at any time it is in play,
- both teams are free to occupy the same area,
- the goal shall be horizontal and elevated.

The game grew rapidly in popularity, the original rules being distributed throughout the world via the YMCA movement. In 1932 the Federation Internationale de Basketball Amateur (FIBA) was formed and it is the rules issued by FIBA that are the official rules for basketball in Britain, the same rules being used by both men and women.

Basketball is an Olympic sport with competition for both men's and women's teams. In Britain local competitions are organised to cater for every standard of play, with National Leagues providing competition for the top players. English teams regularly enter the European Championships that are organised for men and women every two years.

The official rules of the game are written to control the game at international level and the inexperienced person reading the official rules may think basketball a very complex game. This is unfortunate, as basketball is a simple ball-handling game, with a horizontal ring of 18in (45cm) diameter as a target, placed 10ft (3·05m) from the floor at each end of the playing court. The game is played to three basic rules: no contact; one pace whilst holding the ball; and one dribble.

Naismith, when he originally wrote out the rules of the game, listed thirteen rules; over the years since 1891, changes have been made in the rules to define some of Naismith's original rules in greater detail, and to ensure an equal opportunity for each team on both attack and defence. As basketball developed as an international sport, so the rules have become further defined in detail to ensure that when an International game is played disputes are minimal.

Basketball is a game of maximum participation; no player on either team is restricted from getting the ball whenever it is in play, and players are free to occupy any part of the playing area not occupied by an opponent. Each player can shoot from any position on the playing court. The popularity of the game can be traced to this essential simplicity, which enables every player to do everything. Naismith, when he invented the game, wanted a game anyone could play and enjoy. The world-wide popularity of basketball is an indication of his success.

Comments on the No Contact Rule

It is not the intention of the authors in writing this book to offer full instruction on the rules of the game. However, the book would be inadequate if some comments were not made on the no contact rule, which creates the greatest difficulty for officials and players.

It is the duty of every player on court to avoid contact, but it is accepted that with ten players moving rapidly in a confined space contact will occur and the official is charged with the duty of making a judgement on the contact. In a situation where contact occurs the official judges whether the contact is incidental and an acceptable part of the game, or whether to call a foul on the player he judges to have been responsible for causing the contact. Obviously, if a player, due to an error of judgement, tries to play the ball and causes contact in his attempt, then a foul should be called.

Remember that every player on court is entitled to occupy any part of the court not occupied by an opponent, provided that he does not cause any personal contact in obtaining that position. A player is considered to occupy not only the part of the floor covered by his feet, but in addition a 'cylinder' between the floor and the roof with a base roughly equivalent to the player's body dimensions. Should an opponent run or reach into this 'cylinder' and cause contact then he is responsible for that contact. If the player in extending his arm or leg outside his 'cylinder' causes contact, then he is responsible for that contact. It is legal for a player to extend his arm or leg, but should an opponent wish to move by, then the extended limb must be withdrawn.

When players are stationary it is relatively easy to make a correct judgement as to which player is responsible for any contact that may occur, but it is more difficult when the players are moving. The rules of the game differentiate between a dribbler and a player who does not have the ball. A dribbler is expected to be in full control and be able to stop, change direction, pass or shoot in a split second. If you are a dribbler you should expect that defenders will move into your path at any time and you should be prepared to take the action necessary to avoid contact. Until you, as the dribbler, get your head and shoulders past your opponent the greater responsibility for contact remains with you. Once you get your head and shoulders past your defender then greater responsibility for avoiding contact rests with your opponent. Because of this, dribblers should attempt to beat an opponent by driving hard so as to get head and shoulders past the defender. Beware of just throwing the ball forward and causing, and being responsible for, contact as you chase after it.

When you are defending against a dribbler and have established a defensive position in front of him, you may move to force him from his path (without contact); this is good play and referred to as 'defensive steering'. Contact by a dribbler on the front of the defensive player will usually result in the foul being called on the dribbler. Should the contact be by the defender on the side of the dribbler, then the foul should be called on the defensive player. If you find yourself marking a dribbler, providing you can establish a legal defensive position (that is with both feet on the floor and facing the dribbler, in the path of the movement of the dribbler) then should contact occur the dribbler is responsible for this contact. Once you have established your defensive position, the dribbler must be prepared to avoid

9

Fig. 2   Player causing contact by trying to play ball from position of disadvantage

contact. As a defender, providing you gained your position first, you do not have to give the dribbler time and distance in which to stop.

Defending against a player who does not have the ball, you must give a moving opponent time and distance in which to stop or change direction. You may not move into the path of this opponent so quickly that he cannot stop or change direction. This important difference between contact responsibility in relation to a dribbler and a player who does not have the ball should be understood. **Time and distance have no bearing on the situation when a dribbler is involved.**

There will be occasions in a game when a player attempts to shoot or pass with his feet off the floor; in this situation the defender cannot move into the attacking player's path, i.e. into his landing area. As a defender you can continue to move towards an opponent until such time as he leaves the floor. If you are on attack and jumping to shoot or pass against a defender who is stationary before you leave the ground, then if contact occurs the greater responsibility rests with you.

Later in this book a number of screen situations will be covered in some detail, and you should be aware of possible fouls that can occur when setting a screen. A screen occurs when an attacking player attempts to prevent a defender from reaching a desired position or maintaining his defensive position. If the screen is set at the side of, or in front of, a stationary opponent, so that the screener is within the field of vision of the opponent, it can be set at any distance from the opponent short of actual contact. When the screen is set 'blind', that is, out of the opponent's field of vision, the screener must be at least one metre from the opponent. If the screen is being set against a moving opponent, then his speed and direction of movement have to be considered. This means that when screening against a moving opponent the screen should be set one to two metres from the defender.

Once you have set the screen you may only move in the direction and path of your opponent.

Most contact fouls committed in screening situations occur because the screening player moves. If a legal

screen has been set and the opponent is 'picked off' on the screen, then contact is likely to occur and unless the player caught on the screen endeavours to barge his way through, any incidental contact that occurs should be regarded by the official as incidental and an acceptable part of the game.

Equipment

Most basketball clubs make use of playing courts provided in educational establishments or in local sports centres. Not owning their own facilities, they have only a limited influence on the quality of the provision. Some clubs are able to improve their home court through the provision of good quality rings and by regularly maintaining the net in a good condition. The club will need a supply of basketballs to use at training sessions and they should have one better-quality ball for match play. In our opinion clubs should purchase good quality basketballs which offer a longer quality playing life, rather than spend money on the less expensive moulded practice ball. For players who aim to reach a high standard, it is a good idea to purchase a basketball for their own use, and if they have space in their back garden, to fix a practice ring on a wall or post, so they can spend their spare moments shooting. Shooting skill depends a great deal on the time spent shooting a ball at the basket.

Clothing

The individual player's equipment is comparatively simple, the basic playing equipment being shorts and vest. The vest and shorts shown in fig. 3 are ideal, being specially designed for basketball, and permit the maximum freedom of movement. The player will usually be provided with his vest and shorts by his club, so that members of the team wear identical kit, numbered as required by the rules back and front. Clubs will require two sets of playing kit so that there is an alternative colour to wear when there is a colour clash with opponents. Clubs are recommended to have one set in white and one set coloured. Fig. 3 shows the player wearing kit with his club's name attached. Some of the teams playing in the National League supply their players with kit with the club name on the front and the player's name on the back, a useful refinement for the spectator.

Shoes

Footwear is a very important part of the player's equipment. Basketball involves a great deal of running, stopping, changing direction, jumping and landing, and without good comfortable footwear the player could find himself a liability to his team. Basketball shoes are either low cut or high cut, depending upon the personal preference of the player. What is required of a good basketball shoe is that it gives a good grip (on the floor), supports the foot and has a sole thick enough to cushion the jumping and landing that will occur during the game. There are available on the market a number of specialist basketball shoes, some in attractive colours, and the wise player will purchase a quality shoe. A good quality basketball shoe will enhance the player's enjoyment of the game.

Socks

These may be provided by the club, trimmed in the club colours. Players should have a number of pairs of socks available so that they wear clean socks for each basketball session, be it a game or a training session. We recommend the thick cushion-foot type of sock, as they absorb sweat and give an additional cushion for the many landings that the player will make during the game.

Tracksuit

You will need a tracksuit to wear
during warm-up prior to the game and
whilst sitting on the bench as a sub-
stitute. We recommend that the
tracksuit obtained has a full zip in the
jacket and long zips in the legs, so as to
facilitate easy, quick removal.

Bag

The final item of equipment to be
mentioned is a bag for carrying your
kit. In addition to the items already
named, the bag should hold towel
and soap, talcum powder to use on
your feet before dressing, and a spare
set of shoe laces.

Fig. 3   Playing kit

13

Playing positions

The player's position in the team will depend upon his own skill, that of his team-mates, his height in relation to other members of the team and the tactics the coach decides to use. In basketball the name given to the player's position is determined by the area of the court usually taken up when the team is on attack. There are three basic court playing positions: **guard, forward** and **pivot.** These playing areas are illustrated in diag. 1.

Guard

A player who plays in the guard position will, when his team is on attack, usually operate in the area of court between the centre line and the free-throw line extended to the side lines. He will usually be one of the smaller players on the team and will be responsible for bringing the ball up court to start the team's attack. He will need to be a good driver and a capable shooter from the 15–25ft ($4\frac{1}{2}$–$7\frac{1}{2}$m) range from basket. A talented guard will be able to use his drive to move in close to the basket, not necessarily for a shot, but to draw the defence onto himself and then pass off to a team-mate in a better position for the shot. This demands that he is a good passer of the ball and capable of 'reading' the movements of team-mates so as to feed them with

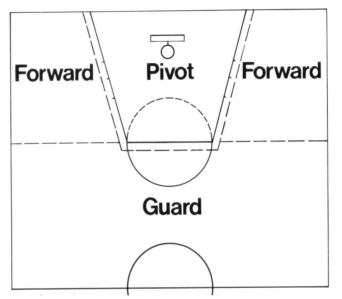

Diagram 1

the ball as they break free. The player who takes the guard position is frequently one of the more experienced players, as from this position he can direct his team's attacking play. For this reason the guard may be referred to as a 'playmaker' or, using an American Football term, a 'quarterback'.

Forward

The forwards play on attack in the area of the court, either on the right- or left-hand side, between the restricted areas and the side lines. They will be among the taller players on the team, have a good drive and be able to shoot well from the corner and side of the court. They must be prepared to set screens to help free a team-mate for a shot. If they are playing forward they must be prepared to move in to gain attacking rebounds should a shot be missed.

Pivot

The player selected to play in the pivot position is usually the tallest player in the team and plays on attack close to the basket. A pivot player will be expected to have the following skills: be a good shot close to basket (usually under pressure from close-marking opponents); have the ability to get free to receive a pass and remain close to the basket and rebound strongly. The player in this position is occasionally referred to as a post player.

These playing positions are by no means rigid and as the team's attacking play develops so a guard may find himself playing from a forward position. However, an inexperienced player will find it easier to understand his role in the team's attack if he is operating from a specific court position.

The number of players that a team uses in each position can be varied, and will depend upon the tactics selected by the team coach. The use of players by the coach will ensure a balanced spacing of the players in their front court. This court balance ensures that players are well spaced out and do not get in each other's way. It may ensure that sufficient players are positioned with responsibility to move in for the attacking rebound and to delay the opponent's outlet pass. One or two players

stationed in the guard position will give defensive cover against possible fast breaks, and be able to receive a pass when an attacking play breaks down.

In basketball a 'shorthand', in which the number of players in each playing position on the court is stated, is used to describe the way the players are organised on attack. For example, an attack with two guards, two forwards, one on each side of the court, and one pivot player, would be referred to as a 2.1.2 formation. This

Diagram 2

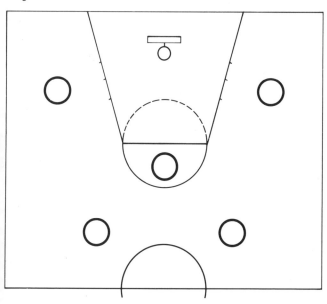

Diagram 3

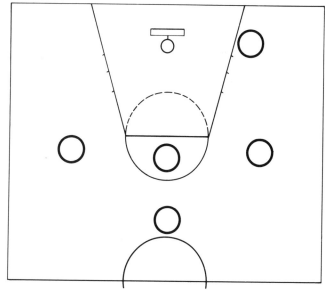

is illustrated in diagram 2. Another commonly used formation is a 1.3.1 formation in which a team plays with one guard, two forwards and two pivot players. This is illustrated in diagram 3. A player must be prepared to occupy any position on court, and should you find yourself playing out of your normal position, you should be aware of the responsibilities of the position in which you find yourself. A guard may well find himself playing in the forward position, and should be aware of his rebound responsibility from this position.

A player can occupy any position on court and will find himself fully involved on attack and defence. This means that on the change of possession he will move with the other players from one end of the court to the other. The defensive position that he takes up will depend upon the defensive tactics being employed by the coach. If he is marking on a man-to-man basis he should be marking an opponent of his own size and ability. If he is playing the pivot position for the team he is likely to find himself marking the opponents' pivot player. Whatever tactics are employed on defence, the team should endeavour to have the tallest players closest to

the basket so that they are in an advantageous position to gain rebounds. After gaining the rebound, they should look for the quick outlet pass to the guards, who will aim to fast break. If the fast break does not result in a shot,

the team should take up their basic attacking formation, and to do this the taller players must overtake the guards who led the fast break, so as to be in a position to operate close to the basket.

Fig. 4   The half-court game

Basic Play

Team play in basketball involves the application of ideas similar to those applied in other team games, for example safe passing, spreading out on attack, movement of the ball and/or player, the pass and the move into an open space for the return pass. An understanding of these ingredients is essential for successful team play and must be considered before individual techniques and skills are analysed in detail.

Use of Space

In the limited area of a basketball court the correct use of space is important. The attacking team will endeavour to spread out so that there is 12–15ft ($3\frac{1}{2}$–$4\frac{1}{2}$m) between each attacking player. At this range, the attacking players can make fast accurate passes; they commit the defenders, making it difficult for one defender to mark two attacking players, or for two defenders to mark the one attacking player with the ball. The attacking team, as they build up their attack, will endeavour to keep the under-basket area free; this is the area where they will be able to score a high percentage of their shots. The defensive team will also be concerned with the use of space and will endeavour to deny the attacking team use of the area of the court where they would be likely to score a high percentage of shots taken. Defensive players will usually station themselves between the man they are marking and the basket they are defending, keeping the attacking players away from the high percentage scoring area. The defensive team will also try to counter any spreading-out by the attacking team by employing tactics that give depth

Fig. 5   Use of space for a shot

to the defence. They will obtain this depth in the defence by 'sagging'. This occurs when a defender moves towards the basket away from the attacking player he is marking. A defender will sag when the opponent he is marking either does not have the ball and is at a distance from the ball handler, or is out of scoring range. Through sagging a defender gives cover and can mark an opponent should he manage to get free near the basket.

Movement

The basic attacking play in basketball should be a pass to a team-mate and a movement towards the basket, looking for a return pass. Beginners and inexperienced players frequently attempt to play the game too fast and make too much movement. Basketball is a game of changes of tempo; play is initially built up slowly and then rapid movement is made as a scoring chance is developed.

Individual Play

The simplest defence used in the game is for a defensive player to be responsible for one opponent, aiming to limit the attacking options of that player. The basic attacking options available to the player are to

shoot, to drive, to pass and to move. Before using any of these options the attacking player may make use of a fake. The basic defensive position should be taken up between the attacking player and the basket that is being defended, so that the attacking player has to dribble round the defender in order to take a close-to-basket shot. The defender will adjust his position, using his hands to discourage an easy shot.

Control

Basketball being a no-contact game, emphasis should be placed on controlled movements about the court. Make a movement only when you have yourself and the ball under control.

Time and Distance

Although the equation
time = distance is not scientific, it forms the basis of an important idea. This is that the time a player has in which to perform a skill will depend upon the distance he is from an opponent, and that the faster he is in reacting to a situation the less distance he will require. A defender marking between the opponent and the basket he is defending will give himself space, so that he has time to

react to the opponent's movement. If he is marking an opponent closely he will find he has less time in which to intercept passes. An important skill of the game is the ability to recognise a game situation as it develops. If the player recognises the situation, he will respond more quickly and will therefore need less space to operate than a player who is slower, or fails to recognise the game situation as it develops. Understanding of the game has been mentioned in the Preface; the player who has superior appreciation of the game has an advantage over the player who has superior technique but lacks the understanding of the game.

Individual Basic Skills

To be a successful basketball player requires the mastery of a number of basic skills. In this book the more important of these skills have been isolated and techniques and basic ingredients discussed. It is important to remember that although the book isolates the particular skills, within the game they are closely interrelated.

Getting Free

In a basic game where defenders are marking individuals in a man-to-man defence, you should expect to be marked by a defender who stands between you and the basket. If you wish to develop as a member of a team it is essential that you learn to free yourself from the defender so that you can receive a pass. A coach may be able to structure certain situations to create scoring chances but ideally the player should also be able to respond to the changing situations as they occur during the game.

Having taken up your attacking position as a guard, forward or pivot, and being within 20 feet of the basket, you should now consider the following:
■ Am I free for a pass? If so, signal for a pass.

■ Is there space nearer the basket to receive a pass?
■ How can I move into that space and be free for a pass?
By assessing the reaction of the defender to certain moves it should be possible to get free.

Backdoor

If the opponent is watching the ball, is it possible to run past him on the outside and get free? Look at fig. 6; with the opponent watching the ball, player no. 6 breaks free towards the basket. This cut on the side of the opponent away from the ball is called a 'backdoor' play.

Remember that as the opponent moves backwards to stay with you, it may be possible to get free by speed alone. An attacking stance, with knees bent, is necessary to make a quick start.

Fig. 6   Defender is watching the ball, and attacking team use a backdoor play

a

b

c

7a

7b

8a

8b

Change of Direction

If the opponent does react to the moves, you can attempt to beat him by using a sudden change of direction. In fig. 7 the attacking player (no. 5) starts to move to his left; as the defender adjusts to cover this move he changes direction, pushing off his outside foot (left foot) to cut inside to the attacking player's right to receive the pass.

A Roll

An alternative method of changing direction is to use a roll. This is shown in fig. 8, where a player attempts to move past his opponent to the outside, in this case to go to the baseline; as the opponent moves to cover, the attacking player stops, pivots on his inside foot and rolls, turning his back on the defender, and breaks to receive a pass.

Fig. 7   Change of direction to get free

Fig. 8   Roll

8c

8d

When trying to get free to receive a
pass, apply the following principles:

■ Stand away from the area in
which you wish to receive the
pass and then move into it for the
pass. Fig. 9 shows a pivot player
stationed on the baseline with the
ball being held by a guard. The
pivot player moves out to the free
throw line to receive the ball.

a

Fig. 9   Baseline player moves out to receive
pass

b

a

b

Stand close, then move away from the basket to receive a pass. The defender will react to movements near to the basket—a step to basket is often sufficient to 'wrong foot' an opponent; you can then move away into space to receive a pass.

The example shown in fig. 10 to illustrate this principle is one of the most commonly-used moves to get free in the game of basketball. The player moves to basket, changes direction and then steps out to receive a pass.

Fig. 10   Player moving to basket and then breaking out to receive a pass

c

Moving Free Against Defensive Pressure

A pivot player may find that he is being 'fronted', i.e. that the defender has taken up a position between him and the ball. When this occurs, the pivot player should step to basket, signalling for a high pass by a team-mate over the defender. In fig. 11 the defender has fronted the pivot player, who steps to basket as his team-mate makes the high overhead pass over two defenders.

Fig. 11   Pivot player, being fronted, moving free to receive a pass

a

b

24

If the defensive pressure is an overplay of the passing lane to a forward at the side of the court, the forward may get free to receive the pass by cutting backdoor as shown earlier, or stepping out to receive the ball at the side. Fig. 12 shows the forward making the latter move, stepping away from the defender to receive the pass at the side of the court.

Fig. 12   Forward steps out to receive a pass

a

b

Creating the Space for the Shooting Chance

Having received the ball within shooting range, if a shot is not immediately possible because of close marking you should move to create space for a shot. Having assessed the situation you may achieve this by simply stepping into a space and shooting. Space may be found in this way at the side or in front of the defender.

Once you have received a pass, endeavour to pivot immediately so as to look for the basket. If, when pivoting, you find that you are within scoring range and the opponent has left you space, you should shoot. Fig. 13 shows the pivot to face the basket, thus creating a 'triple threat' situation; the player can **shoot**, **dribble** or **pass.**

Fig. 13   Face the basket and if space shoot

26

a

b

Once you have pivoted to face the
basket, if the defender is not in line
between you and the basket, but is still
close to you, you should drive for
basket for your shot.

c

27

Having received the ball within
shooting range, you may find yourself
closely marked but to one side. By
stepping past the opponent you create
space so that you may move in for the
shot. In fig. 15 the attacking player, as
he turns to face the basket, finds his
opponent close but to one side, so he
steps past the defender and drives for
basket.

Fig. 15   Drive past the opponent for basket

a

b

Another method of creating space for
the shot is to jump and shoot. Timing is
obviously important and a fake may be
necessary before you go for the shot,
so that the defender is not in a position
to interfere with it. Fig. 16 shows a
player 'fading' slightly away from the
opponent in addition to jumping and
shooting. This requires a high level of
shooting skill, as the fade places the
shooter slightly off-balance in the
shot.

c

Fig. 16   Player jumping and shooting

a

Fig. 17   Pivot player turning and shooting

A pivot player will frequently receive a pass with his back to the basket. Upon reception of the ball he should look over his shoulder to see where his opponent is stationed.

If the defender has sagged, the pivot player should pivot and shoot.

The pivot player may receive the ball close to basket and find the defender

b

c

Fig. 18   *Pivot player stepping past opponent and driving for basket*

over-playing one side. If this happens, he should jump through the space left vacant to lay the ball up on the backboard. This is illustrated in fig. 40. If the pivot player is some way from basket when he finds that he is being over-played on one side, he should step hard to basket past the opponent and drive in for a closer shot.

b

Signalling

Signalling is vital if the player is to develop an understanding with the ball handler. It tells the latter not only that the player is free for a pass but also, if correctly executed, where and when the player wishes to receive the ball. A signal may be executed with one or two hands, the fingers being extended and spread to give a large target.

Develop the habit, when on attack, of constantly signalling for the ball. Fig. 19 shows a guard offering his team-mate with the ball a good signal. Notice that this signal is made to his side away from the defender.

When moving across court or towards the basket, a player should normally signal with the leading hand—if possible away from the defender. The signal should lead the player through on a cut to basket, as it does for the guard in fig. 20.

The pivot player, when moving away from the basket towards the ball handler, should try to signal with both hands. In fig. 21 a pivot player, moving out to set a post position at the free throw line, signals with both hands.

19

20

Fig. 19   Signal for the ball
Fig. 20   Guard cutting and signalling for a pass
Fig. 21   Pivot player signals with two hands for a pass

Passing the Ball

When passing the ball the player's first consideration should be to make a safe pass. The safe passing range is usually considered to be between 12 and 15ft ($3\frac{1}{2}$–$4\frac{1}{2}$m) unless there is a large space available free of opponents in which to receive the pass. Signalling by team members provides a target, tells the ball handler they are ready to receive the ball and may help him to decide on the direction and timing of the pass. However, the player must still consider his own defender, who will be trying to prevent the pass. Just because a team-mate signals, the ball handler does not have to pass—he must make the final decision as to whether it is possible to pass.

When you have the ball, try to assess each situation as it develops, considering the following:

- How far away is the team-mate; is he stationary or moving? Remember the distance/time relationship—the longer distance passes give opponents more time to move in and intercept.
- How far away is the opponent? If he is close, he will have less time to move his hands to intercept the pass; the farther away he is, the more time he has for the interception.

21

- Can the pass requested by the team-mate's signal be made?
- Is an alternative pass possible and more productive?

A skilled passer should try to be deceptive, disguise his intentions by looking well ahead, and develop a poker face. Try not to stare at the receiver. Pass the ball quickly and firmly; quick release is preferable to fast, hard movement through the air. The fast pass may involve a preparatory wind-up that will give the opponent a chance to anticipate the pass, and it may also be difficult for the team-mate to catch. Passes must be sympathetic. Whenever possible, try to pass in a horizontal plane.

Chest Pass

This pass is used when there is space, and speed is required. In fig. 22 the pass is being used against a zone defence, speed being important as the aim is to out-manoeuvre an opponent to create a shooting opportunity.

22

23

Fig. 22   Chest pass being used against a zone defence

Fig. 23   Chest pass being used in a demonstration at the end of a fast break

34

Overhead Pass

Guards and forwards should practise using the overhead pass—it is a quick alternative to a shot and is particularly valuable for short passing situations when closely marked, and for making a pass over a smaller opponent. Pivot players should be expert in using this pass when unable to penetrate the defence and go for a shot. Against a pressing defence the pivot player has space to operate above head height, which may be difficult to defend. The pivot player receiving an overhead pass can help break a pressure defence.

Fig. 24 shows the overhead pass being used to pass the ball in to a pivot player who has taken up a post position.

Bounce Pass

This pass should only be used when a horizontal pass is not possible. It is used in a close passing situation, as illustrated in fig. 25, or in a situation against a close-marking opponent who has his arms up and may be bigger than the passer.

24

25

Fig. 24   Overhead pass

Fig. 25   Bounce pass being used in close situation

35

Passing to a Cutting Player

When passing to a cutting player, remember that your team-mate wants the ball ahead of him so that he can run on to it. He does not want to have to check his movement; if he does, the defender he has beaten could well have time to recover.

Other Passes

The majority of the passes so far considered are two-hand passes that will be used at the 12–15ft ($3\frac{1}{2}$–$4\frac{1}{2}$m) range. A player's repertoire of passes increases as his game develops, and may include, for example, the one-hand pass being used in fig. 27 to start a fast break, or the short range pass being used in fig. 28 in a screen situation.

26

27

Fig. 26   Pass ahead of a cutting player

Fig. 27   One-hand pass used to start a fast break

36   Fig. 28   Short range pass

Receiving a Pass

When receiving the ball, reach out to meet the ball early, 'giving' with the hands to help absorb the force of the pass. It may be necessary to catch and protect the ball; if so, hold the ball firmly but turn it so that one hand is above and one below it. The arms and hands will then protect the ball from an underhand slap. This also enables the ball to be pressed firmly into the shooting hand. Do not pull the ball in close to the body—in this position it is difficult to make a quick pass and easier for an opponent to tie you up and gain a held ball.

If you are facing the basket when you receive a pass, you should immediately look for basket, and shoot if you are close enough and have enough space.

Footwork
The Stop and Pivot

Having established that it is necessary for a player to move away from his defender to get free for a pass, it is likely that he will still be moving when he receives the ball. To satisfy the rules of the game it is essential to learn to stop without travelling.

There are two ways of stopping on receiving a pass; which method you

Fig. 29   Player, having received a pass, protecting the ball

will use will usually depend on the game situation.

Stride Stop

This is performed using a 'one, two' rhythm. The ball is received with the feet off the floor; one foot touches the floor, then the other. Fig. 30 shows a player landing first on his right foot and then on his left, as he uses a 'one, two' (right, left) rhythm to come to a

stop. To prevent further forward movement the stopping stride should be longer than normal and the floor should be contacted with a flat-footed action, with the knees bent.

Fig. 30   Stride stop

a

b

c

The Jump Stop

This is particularly valuable if a player is moving away from the basket when he receives the ball. In fig. 31 the player moving out to set a post at the free throw line uses a jump stop as he receives the ball from a guard. Note the jump prior to receiving the ball, and the flexing of the knees as he lands with feet parallel and flat. In this stop emphasis should be laid on the simultaneous landing of both feet, the player having taken the ball with both feet off the floor. This stop is valuable in that there is no commitment to a pivot foot on landing. As the landing has been made on both feet simultaneously, either foot may be selected to be the pivot foot, depending upon the game situation. This stop will be used when a player is moving towards the basket to take a jump shot; in this situation one foot is usually slightly ahead of the other, the same foot forward as the shooting hand.

The jump stop is sometimes referred to as a 'scoot' stop.

a

Fig. 31   Jump stop

Pivoting

The pivot is closely linked with stopping, as the type of stop used will influence the variety of pivot options available. If the jump stop can be mastered, it has the advantage of giving a choice of pivot foot, enabling the player to move either the left or right foot to take advantage of a particular situation. The stride stop, however, will restrict the options as you can only pivot on the 'one' count foot, usually the rear foot.

Time must be spent practising the use of the pivot to move round an opponent using a dribble, or to create space for a shot.

A forward who has moved out to receive a pass should, if **loosely marked,** turn inwards (towards the centre of the court) by pivoting on his right foot, at the same time moving his left foot into the normal shooting position, with knees flexed and slightly apart; this will enable him to shoot or drive towards the basket. If **closely marked,** by performing a rear pivot he may be able to step past his defender on the 'outside', creating space for a base-line drive.

Shooting

Having created space for a shot, it is essential to be able to score consistently. It has already been established that it is vital to look for a shot early. However, because the target is an empty space it is important to select a point as near to that space as possible. When making an 'off the board' shot, commonly used for lay-up and hook shots, focus on a spot within or near to the rectangle above the basket. In other shots select a point on the rim; personal preference will help you to choose whether this is the front or rear edge, and once it has been decided, always aim at the same place during practice so that it becomes habitual.

Regular practice is essential to obtain accuracy in shooting. Since most practice will not take place in the presence of the coach, it is important for players to understand some of the principles which will affect the accuracy of their shots.

To develop a high level of concentration, practise shooting under conditions as near as possible to those found in the game. The ritual seen as a player prepares to take a free shot, the adjustment of the feet and bouncing of the ball, is an attempt to stimulate relaxation and confidence, the foundations for which have been laid during practice. During the game it is necessary to shoot under conditions of physical and mental stress. Your opponents will constantly be trying to distract you and discourage you from taking an accurate shot. So whenever possible practise against an opponent; the adjustments necessary to counter defensive moves will help to improve your timing and develop speed of shot, so important if you are to take advantage of defensive errors.

During practice concentrate on the following:

- Look for your shot early—concentrate on the rim before, during, and after the shot.

- Hold the ball firmly in both hands with fingers spread.

- Shoot with one hand—the wrist of the shooting hand should be fully extended before the shot; this is achieved by applying pressure with the non-shooting hand.

- Shoot with a strong wrist and finger flick—the follow-through with the wrist will then give a natural back-spin to the ball as it leaves the fingers.

- Be on balance and under control during the shot—this enables a smooth follow-through which is essential for accuracy. Balance starts at the feet, so always establish a firm foot position before shooting.

The shot to be used will largely depend on how the player has created or made use of space. The basic shots are illustrated, with comments on each shooting action. As players develop their game, they establish their own style of shooting based upon these basic shooting actions. At the end of a dribble, having escaped from the defender, a player would normally use a lay-up shot if close to the basket.

Fig. 32   Shot being taken in game

Fig. 33   A lay-up shot being used at the end o a fast break

42

32

33

Lay-up Shot

This shot should be mastered by all players, as it forms the basis from which different shooting styles can be developed for close-to-basket shots. The essential ingredients of the shot are that it is taken on the move, usually on the run, the player jumps up and towards the basket as he shoots, and stretches to release the ball as close to the basket as possible. As you move forward and pick the ball up at the end of a dribble (as illustrated in fig. 34), or after receiving a pass, hold the ball firmly in your hands, lifting your head as you gather the ball so that you can look for the shot early. The illustration of the ball being taken in the air shows the player landing first on his right foot and then on his left foot, as he takes a long final step. This enables him to control his forward momentum and helps him to prepare for the high jump off the left foot. As he jumps off one foot, he carries the ball upwards, still in both hands. Notice that the take-off foot for the shot is the opposite to the shooting hand. The player releases the ball at full stretch from one hand, using the backboard to bank the ball into the basket.

f

44

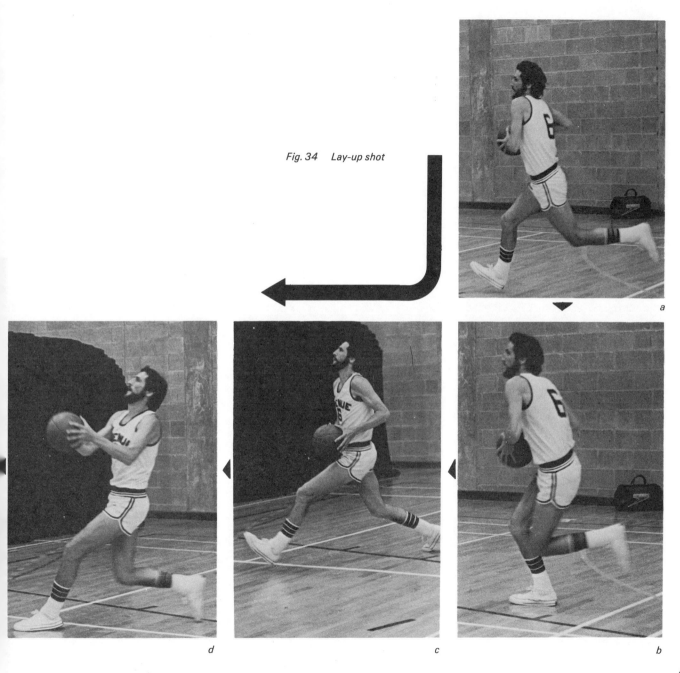

Fig. 34   Lay-up shot

a

b

c

d

Set Shot

Although this shot has limited use in the modern game it may be used for distance shots should the defender sag off. It is sometimes used when shooting over a front screen (see fig. 35), but is most commonly used when taking a free throw. Fig. 36 shows a player using a set shot from the free throw line.

Notice that the player taking the set shot takes up a stride position with his feet, the same foot forward as his shooting hand. Prior to taking the shot he bends his knees slightly. If he had been taking this shot during the normal course of play he would be using a basic attacking stance that involves a similar position with the feet

and with slight flexion of the knees. The player looks at the basket throughout the shot. He follows through with a vigorous snap of the wrist and fingers, and with the powerful drive from the legs finishes the shot at full stretch.

Fig. 35   Set shot being used over a front screen

Fig. 36   Player taking a free throw using a set shot

47

Jump Shot

This is perhaps the most effective shot in the modern game. When used in conjunction with a fake it is a very difficult shot to defend, unless your opponent has a considerable height advantage. The shot may be from a stationary position following a head or foot fake, after a pivot, after receiving a pass, or at the end of a

e

d

c

dribble. When developing the jump shot, you must learn to take this shot following a jump stop and from a stride stop at the end of the dribble. Try to take off from both feet and jump vertically, attempting to release the ball when in an almost stationary position, near the top of the jump. The timing of the jump should enable you to avoid defensive attempts to intercept the shot. The timing of your shot during the jump is also important (see variations of basic technique, page 53). Fig. 37 shows a player taking a jump shot. He uses a stride stop, turning as he stops to face the basket. He jumps from two feet, taking the ball up in front of the face to be held above the forehead. Now he concentrates on the basket and near the top of his jump releases the ball with an upwards extension of the arms, flipping the ball towards the basket with a vigorous wrist and finger action. Notice the carriage of the ball in two hands with the shooting hand behind the ball.

Fig. 37   Jump shot

b

a

Hook Shot

This is a shot pivot players should try to master. It is used when close to the basket and is particularly valuable if the ball is received when the player has his back to the basket, as the body can be used to protect the shooting arm from opponents.

Fig. 38 shows a player having received the ball with his back to the basket. Notice how he looks over his shoulder to establish where his opponent is stationed. He then steps away, looking early for the basket, continuing to hold the ball firmly in both hands. This step is made onto the opposite foot to the shooting hand. The player jumps off this foot, reaching and stretching for the shot, which is completed with a flick of the wrist and fingers. When he turns to look at the target, he picks a spot on the backboard and endeavours to hit this spot with a 'soft' shot. The follow-through he has made after the shot brings him facing the basket and into a good position to move for a rebound. Practise taking this shot with either hand; in this way you will be difficult to defend.

a

b

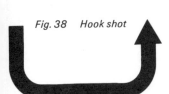

Fig. 38   Hook shot

d

c

Fig. 39 Hook lay-up shot

Other Shots

Mention has been made that players will develop variations of the basic shooting techniques. An example of this is a **hook-lay**. This is used when a player, driving for basket, finds that an opponent has allowed him to move close to basket, but has prevented a clear lay-up shot. In this situation the player would use the footwork of the lay-up shot, but instead of taking the ball up in front of the face as expected, take it up to the side away from the opponent and use a hook shot action to shoot the ball

Fig. 40 Slide shot

40a

softly over his head towards the target.

This hook lay-up shot may involve the player moving slightly away from the target as he shoots, something that would not be encouraged with beginners. However, as beginners develop their game and gain greater control over their shooting, they should consider developing a jump shot in which they fade away from their opponent **slightly**, thus creating space for the shot.

A shot useful to develop for close-to-basket play is a shot that is a cross between a lay-up shot and a jump shot; see fig. 40, the **slide shot.** The attacking player finds that the defender has allowed him space under the basket, and rather than stepping through the gap the player jumps through the space created, to lay the ball against the backboard and score. This shot has the advantage that should the player be fouled and prevented from scoring he will be awarded two free throws, as he is in his shooting action from the moment he moves. If he were to dribble through the space and be fouled while dribbling, his team would only be awarded the ball at the side line, because a player is not in the act of shooting until he has picked the ball up from the dribble.

0b

40c

The Dribble

It is essential to learn to dribble if you are to realise your potential as a player. Because the dribble enables a player to move with the ball it increases his mobility when he is attacking. Try not to waste this asset by aimlessly bouncing the ball.

Remember that before a dribble you are 'alive' and may move anywhere, but after your dribble you are 'dead' and may not dribble again. Before using the dribble you are a 'triple threat', being able to pass, shoot or dribble, and this creates problems for your defender. After your dribble you may pass or shoot but have lost your option of moving with the ball and are easier to defend.

Try to master the following to improve dribbling:

- Control the ball by spreading the fingers comfortably, so that they contact as much of the ball as possible.
- Push the ball down firmly using hand, elbow and wrist.
- Your hand should be on top of the ball. This will prevent 'palming' and ensure that the ball rebounds back to the hand accurately.
- Always hold your head up; be able to see your team-mates.

- The force of the ball as it rebounds from the floor should be absorbed by the fingers, wrist and arm. **Do not** bat or slap the ball.
- Be able to dribble with either hand.
- Learn to stop at the end of your dribble to prevent 'travelling' or fouls being called.
- Learn to change the speed of your dribble, be able to stop and start quickly.
- Beware of being 'double teamed' by your opponents.
- Beware of the single bounce dribble. It is a bad habit that will reduce your effectiveness as an attacker.

The Dribble as a Weapon in Attack

The dribble is used extensively by a guard when bringing the ball up court (see fig. 41). When there is no opposition, he should bounce the ball high in front of his body; this enables him to concentrate on the situation ahead. His approach may be fast or slow, and he should look for opportunities to pass or shoot.

When challenged by a defender, it may be necessary to protect the ball (see fig. 42). The knees should be bent, the dribble lowered and the ball brought to the side of the body. The non-dribbling arm and foot will give additional protection.

The dribble may be used to draw the defender before making a pass. An attacker may dribble into a space

Fig. 41   Guard bringing ball up court

Fig. 42   Dribbler protecting ball

41

42

near the basket and as defenders move to adjust their defensive positions to cover the threat, they may leave a space into which a team-mate may move, signal and receive a pass. Defenders will frequently overplay the dribbling hand and attackers can make use of this fact to create a passing lane to a team-mate. During a fast break, if speed is essential it must be controlled. Attackers should use a high dribble, so that they can adopt a normal running posture, using a pumping action of the arms so that the ball rebounds in front of the body. When attackers find themselves playing against a man-to-man full court pressing defence, a useful way to beat the defence is to give the ball to the best dribbler and to clear out of his way, so he can bring the ball down court against one defender as in fig. 44.

fig. 44

Fig. 43   Dribble being used in fast break

43

45a

45b

Against a zone press, use of the dribble may be to the defensive team's advantage, so passing would be used to beat the zone press.

The Drive

This occurs when a dribble is attempted straight to the basket. If the defender covers this move, try changing the direction of the dribble to take advantage of the space on the other side.

Fig. 45 shows a player dribbling to his left; as the defender adjusts his position to cover this move, the attacking player switches the ball to the right hand in front of his body, at the same time driving hard off the left foot, to change his direction and take advantage of space created on the other side of the defender.

Fig. 44   Dribble being used against a man-to-man pressing defence

Fig. 45   Change hands and change direction on the dribble to beat an opponent

44

45c

45d

Reverse Dribble

Another method of beating an opponent who overplays your dribbling hand is to use a reverse dribble. This move is similar to the 'change hands and change direction', except that as fig. 46 shows, the dribbler pivots and turns his back on his opponent, thus rolling round and past the defender. This move should be used when the defensive player is too close for the attacker to switch dribbling hands across in front of the body. For example, when dribbling with the left hand to the right-hand side of the defender, as the latter adjusts to cover, the dribbler should check his movement, executing a stride stop. As he pivots on his front foot, he should change his dribbling hand, rolling with his back to the defender, and completing the drive to the defender's left. As the dribbler

rolls, it is important that he takes a long step past the opponent.

A guard, when bringing the ball down court against a close-marking defender, may use a number of reverses to force the defender to retreat. This movement is sometimes referred to as backing the defender up, and the dribbler will use a side-stepping shuffle, constantly changing hands to protect the ball.

Fig. 46   Reverse dribble

Changes of Speed and Rhythm

During any dribble sequence, changes of speed and rhythm may be sufficient to give the dribbler the half pace advantage necessary to get him free. Good footwork is essential during the dribble as it enables the player to stop and change direction whilst maintaining good balance. Learn to stop at the end of a dribble using either a stride or a jump stop. Having come to a stride stop because further forward movement is stopped by a defender, look for an opportunity to pivot on your rear foot to make space for a shot, or to protect the ball as you make space for a pass.

A useful move to develop is a dribble in which the initial movement is made at some speed. The defender's reaction to this will be to retreat. You should then execute a stop,

a   b   c

58

Using a Dribble to Manoeuvre an Opponent into a Screen

but keep the dribble going; as the defender checks his backwards movement and tightens up on you (i.e. moves closer to you), try to accelerate past him. You will find this hesitation dribble a useful addition to your dribbling skills.

Fig. 47 shows a player using a screen to help him lose a close-marking opponent. The dribbler backs the defender up to the screen, using a shuffling action with the feet; he then reverses, pivoting close to the team-mate who has established the screen.

The dribbler moves free, taking a clear jump shot to score.

*Fig. 47
Dribbler using a
screen to get free*

a

e

b

c

d

a

b

c

d

Dribbler Creating Screen for Team-mate

When a dribbler's forward progress is blocked by a defender, a quick stop and pivot away from the defender may create a screen situation for a team-mate to use. In fig. 48 a team-mate uses the screen for a jump shot. If the team-mate who uses the dribbler as a screen had been closely marked, he could have moved in such a way as to 'brush' the defender off on the dribbler who has been forced to stop.

Individual Attacking Play with the Ball

Upon receiving the ball close to the basket, a player should always look for his shot before considering a dribble. This will help him to assess his defender's position. Normally the latter will be positioned between the attacker and the basket, preventing a straight drive to goal. There is now a 'cat and mouse' situation. Can the defender be moved away from this position to create space for a drive? Try to make him move forwards, upwards, sideways or backwards and thus force him to make a defensive error of judgement.

Forward Movement by the Defender

As a player turns to face the basket, and looks to see if he can shoot, his opponent may be tempted to move towards him to pressure his shot. As the defender moves forward, step past him and drive for basket.

Fig. 49   Drive past defender moving forward

a

b

c

Fig. 48   Dribbler stopping, pivoting and being used as a screen by a team-mate

50a

50b

51a

51b

Upward Movement by the Defender

As an attacking player you may fake to shoot, by lifting the ball and your shoulders slightly. Should your opponent then jump up to prevent the shot, there will be space to drive past him for the basket. This move is occasionally called 'up and under'.

50c

Fig. 50   Drive past defender jumping to check face shot

Sideways Movement by the Defender

Provided an attacker has not used his dribble, he may force the defender into making the mistake of moving sideways in response to a fake step before the dribble. In fig. 51 the attacking player fakes to start his dribble to the right by making a step in that direction; as the defender moves to cover, the attacker steps again with his right foot across his opponent, driving to basket with his left hand. Throughout the fake step the player uses his left foot as his pivot foot. When using this move, remember that the rules require that your pivot foot must remain grounded until you release the ball at the start of your dribble.

51c

Fig. 51   Drive past defender moving laterally **63**

Fig. 52   Fake drive and shot as the defender steps backwards

a

Backwards Movement by the Defender

As already suggested, a skill to be developed is the stride stop, to be used at the end of a dribble, pivoting on the rear foot to make space for a shot. This movement can be used on receiving the ball; if the attacker fakes to drive by stepping towards the basket, then as the defender steps backwards to cover, the attacker can pivot away from him and shoot. This movement is sometimes called a 'rocker step'. Fig. 52 shows a player faking to drive and stepping back to shoot as the defender retreats. Obviously, as the attacking player pivots back to take the shot the defender may move forward to cover, leaving an opportunity for the attacking player to drive for basket.

b

c

Individual Defence

Individual defence based upon sound 'man-to-man' principles is essential for good team defence.

A player's responsibilities in defence against an individual opponent may be listed as follows:

- Discourage your opponent from shooting from a high percentage scoring area.

- Anticipate his moves so as to discourage him from driving past you for a shot from closer to basket.

- Make it difficult for him to pass accurately, particularly passes into the high percentage scoring area.

- Prevent him from running past you to receive a pass or collect a rebound.

- Perform the above without committing a foul.

Defensive Position

Initially the defensive position will be 'in line' between the opponent and the basket. If the opponent is in a shooting position, the defender should be close enough to discourage the shot; should the opponent be away from the ball, the defender can sag off him towards the basket he is defending, changing his stance so as to be able to see the opponent and the ball.

Fig. 53   Individual defence

Footwork

The basic defensive position which has been recommended cannot be static, or the opponent will be able to move past. To prevent penetration by a cutting or driving player, learn to move backwards quickly. This may seem an unnatural movement, but with practice and hard work the skill can be developed. Good individual defence is based upon the use of the feet; the stance taken up must be one that will facilitate movement. Adopt a low position, one foot in front of the other, knees bent, hips slightly flexed, and move with your opponent using a basic shuffle sliding action with the feet. Should it be necessary to run to regain a defensive position against an opponent, you should use a normal sprinting action.

The basic stance is maintained when moving forwards towards an opponent, perhaps in an attempt to discourage a shot. In this situation beware of moving too quickly. Remember his attacking options, and that the closer you are to him the less time there will be to react to his movements. So don't get too close, and don't jump; retain your low position and contact with the floor, as this will enable you to change direction quickly.

Before a dribble the opponent is 'alive', so adopt a wide stance, using the forward hand to discourage the shot if he is in range, and try to anticipate his moves. With the right foot forward, defending will be easy if your opponent tries to penetrate to your left, as you just move your left foot back to cover his move, then shuffle to stay with him. If he tries to go to your right you have to step back with your right foot and then shuffle to cover his move.

Use of the Arms and Hands

The arms should be flexed and hands carried at about shoulder height, with the palms of the hands facing the ball, and arms flexed to enable quick movement in any direction. When playing against a dribbler, keep your hands low, so that should the dribbler make an error and fail to protect the ball with his body you can attempt to steal the ball. This would be done with an upward movement of the hands. Using the hands in this manner is less likely to result in a foul or to move the defender off balance. Quick hands and vigorous movements of the arms are essential to good defence. The 'windmill' action of the arms may be used effec-

tively to discourage an accurate pass, particularly at an out-of-bounds situation.
The hands are particularly valuable for feeling for screens when a player is moving backwards.

Defending Against a Dribbler

Fig. 54 shows the bent knees stance and use of shuffling action with the feet to cover the movement of the dribbler. This stance enables the defender to move quickly across court to stay between the opponent and the basket. Using this 'boxer's shuffle', a player is able to change direction quickly.

If the basic 'in line position' is adjusted so that the dribbling hand can be overplayed, it may be possible to prevent the opponent from penetrating to a good shooting position. In this way, by thinking about the opponent's play, it may be possible to force him to use his weaker hand. In fig. 54 the defender is covering the direction in which the dribbler wishes to move.

Should the opponent gain an advantage, break from the shuffle step and run at full speed to regain the defensive position between the opponent and the basket. Head directly towards the basket to be defended as

a

b

Fig. 54   Marking a dribbler   67

attacking players frequently go on a curve to basket, and a straight run could well take you to basket ahead of your opponent.

After a dribble your opponent is 'dead' and you should learn to react quickly to this situation. If he is within shooting range, as in fig. 55, move in to a close range with both hands up to prevent the shot. You are safe in taking this close position because the attacking player cannot dribble. You should take up a stance with feet wide spread so as to discourage the opponent from stepping past for the shot. If the opponent is outside shooting range, you can either sag off and attempt to intercept his pass—if the arms are kept up a penetrating pass may be discouraged—or move in close to pressure him into an error or tie the ball up. Which option is used will depend upon your assessment of the opponent and the tactics the coach has given on defence. Fig. 56 shows a team using a sagging defence.

Defence Off the Ball

When a player is marking away from the ball, adjustments to the 'in line' principle may be necessary, so that he can see his opponent and the ball. A strict 'in line' defence may leave spaces in the defence near to the ball. By slightly adjusting to an 'off line' position, it may be possible for a team to cover potential scoring areas. This movement to fill spaces towards the ball is sometimes called floating.

Thinking on Defence

Good individual defence is played with the two ends of the body, the feet and the brain. The feet are used to maintain a defensive position, the brain to work out what the attacking opponent may do. Once you have brought your brain into action to help you defend you can use your hands and arms usefully. If you have heart and are prepared to take pride in your defensive ability you will be a very useful member of any basketball team.

Try to analyse your opponent's moves, his strengths and weaknesses:

■ Is he a good dribbler; can he use either hand?

■ Does he shoot; what is his range?

■ When he drives does he always go the same way?

■ Does he bounce the ball before every shot?

■ Does he signal and move to free himself for a shot?

■ Does he use the same fake every time?

■ Does he react to a defensive fake? If you fake to steal the ball will he stop his dribble?

Answers to these questions should enable you to anticipate possible moves and help you to reduce your opponent's potential as an attacking player. Re-read the list of possible mistakes by defenders (see p. 61) and remember that as a defender you aim not to make these mistakes. Don't rush forward, don't jump up; when a player sets off to dribble past you don't move laterally, step back; don't move too far away from an opponent who is a capable shooter.

◀ Fig. 55   *Close-marking a player who has used his dribble*

▼ Fig. 56   *Sagging defence*

Overplaying to Discourage a Pass

An attacking player in the high percentage scoring area can easily be prevented from scoring if the defender overplays him to discourage a pass. Instead of sagging off the opponent, the defender adjusts his position so that he is to the side of the opponent nearest the ball, thus overplaying the pass. He has one hand up to discourage the pass, and the other hand touching the opponent to ensure that he is alert to any movement that may be made. When a team defensive tactic is to overplay all passes by defensive players adjusting from the basic man-to-man defence position, it is called a pressing defence.

57

Fig. 57   Overplaying a pass to a forward

Fig. 58   Overplaying a pass to a pivot player

Blocking Out and Rebounding

By reading the opponent's moves, it should be possible for a defender to maintain an inside defensive position, so essential if he is to get a rebound. When marking a player who is some way from the basket, watch him closely when the shot goes up, sagging off to prevent him from run-

70

58

ning past you, then block him out by pivoting into his path using a front or rear pivot, depending upon the space between yourself and the opponent. Fig. 59 shows a defensive player blocking out white no. 5 shooting from close to basket. Note that he establishes a strong blocking out position, getting the player he is blocking out on his back. This strong position enables the defender to resist contact; if he did not, he would be liable to be pushed underneath the basket into a bad rebounding position. The player blocking out has his knees bent and feet wide apart, with the arms carried at shoulder height, so they can be used to help lift him up for the rebound.

Having blocked out, the defender should now be in a position from which he can time his jump and go for the rebound. When going for the rebound, he reaches up for the ball with both hands, trying to time his jump so that he catches the ball at full stretch. Inexperienced players frequently jump too early for a rebound and find they have landed again before the ball reaches them. Learn to time your jump; it is useful advice not to go up for the rebound until you see the ball leave the backboard or ring.

a

b

Fig. 59   Blocking out and rebounding

Rebounding in Attack

As an attacking player you will find it more difficult to obtain the inside position at a rebound situation. You should look for the defender turning to watch the ball as the shot goes up, and then cut into the gap under the basket. To prevent yourself being blocked out, you could try using a feint to help create space for a rebound. If you obtain a position in front of the backboard, close enough to be able to make a vertical jump for the ball, you will be less likely to foul. Go for the ball with two hands, watching the ball closely.

Tall players or good jumpers may be able to tip the missed shot back into the basket. In the tip shot, the ball should be cushioned momentarily on the fingers (so the player gains control) before being flicked towards the basket. Should a player gain an attacking rebound and not be able to tip the ball back into the basket, he should take the ball in two hands as he comes back to the ground and immediately try to go straight back up for a shot.

Fig. 60   Tip-in shot

Principles of Team Attack

Most basketball instructional books give details of a particular team attack that could be used. In this book, rather than teach one attacking play, material will be covered that forms a basis for any team attack.

Aim

The basic aim of the attacking team is to retain possession of the ball until they create an opportunity for a good shot. There will occasionally be times when the subsidiary aim of retaining possession and consuming time is more important, for example when a team is one point in the lead and there are only 25 seconds left to play in the game. As the rules require a shot within 30 seconds, the team only need to retain possession to win and should under no circumstances shoot. Even uncontested lay-up shots have been missed, and while a team has possession the opponents cannot score.

Use of Space

Throughout the book a number of references have been made to the use of space. In the use of space as an ingredient of team attack, what is important is the space between attacking team-mates. This space will be influenced by the good passing range of 12–15ft ($3\frac{1}{2}$–$4\frac{1}{2}$m). At this range, attacking team-mates can make quick safe passes and the defensive team is forced to mark on a one-to-one basis, i.e. one defender cannot mark more than one attacking player. This space between attacking team-mates will give the player with the ball room to drive to basket without having to cope with more than one defender, and assists not only with driving plays but also with cutting plays. This good passing range could be looked upon as a 'support' range, in that team-mates at this range support each other, but note that because basketball is a fast passing game the attacking formations mentioned earlier in the book create situations where some players on court support team-mates who do not have the ball. This is good, as it keeps the defensive players occupied and places the attacking players in a good position should the ball be passed. The three lane fast break discussed later is a good example of attacking players supporting each other at this basic range. This range could be looked upon as a divergent situation on attack, with screen plays being the convergent situation. These situations should be strictly maintained by the attacking team, and players should not operate in the 'no-man's-land' between having a screen set and being at the good passing range.

Threat

Ideally a player on attack in his front court should, when he receives a pass, be a scoring threat. Should he move out of scoring range he will become less of a threat to the defenders and so easier to mark. Another point to mention under the heading 'threat' is that the attacking team should endeavour to penetrate the defence by moving the ball or players towards the basket. This penetration can create problems for the defensive team; for example, the player who is marking the attacking player who has passed in may not be able to see both his opponent and the ball. The movement that the attacking team uses will create scoring chances and the form that the movement takes could depend upon the defence being employed, with emphasis on player movement against a man-to-man defence, and upon ball movement when playing against a zone defence. These are emphasised because situations will

Organisation

occur when player movement is the most appropriate method of creating a scoring chance against a zone defence.

The amount of organisation in a team's attacking play will depend upon their coach. He may wish them to use patterns of play that they have learnt during training sessions, or he may give them a basic formation and want them to play freely from these positions. These extremes of approach have some limitations; playing freely, for example, makes it more difficult for all members of the team to know what is happening.

Fig. 61   Creating space for a good shot

Creating Scoring Opportunities

Three basic methods of creating a scoring opportunity can be isolated. These are:

- The player with the ball manoeuvres to free himself for a shot.
- A player without the ball moves free and then receives a pass and shoots.
- A screen situation is used to enable an attacking player to lose the defender who is responsible for marking him.

The first method has already been discussed under the heading 'Individual Attack with the Ball'. The second method, in which a player gets free to receive a pass from a team-mate with the ball, is illustrated under the *Give and Go* and *Backdoor* plays. These are two-man plays used to get a player free when he does not have the ball. A screen occurs when an attacking player attempts to prevent an opponent from reaching a desired position or maintaining his defensive position. The object of the screen is to impede the progress of the defender so that the attacking player he is marking has an unobstructed shot or a clear path to basket. A number of screen situations that players should

be able to recognise and create have been illustrated in this book.

Although a basketball team consists of five players on court, it is usually through the efforts of two and occasionally three players combining that one player is freed for a shot. This is not to imply that the players not involved have no task—they must keep the defenders occupied so that they cannot help out. In a fast-moving game like basketball, you may find yourself creating space for a team-mate at one moment and trying to work with a team-mate to free one of you for a shot the next.

Fig. 62   Two-versus-two play is often the basis of the attacking team's effort to create a scoring opportunity

Give and Go

In this move you do just that—Give the ball to a team-mate, then Go to basket looking for a return pass. Any two players on court can work together in this way, with a player taking advantage of a mistake by his opponent to cut free, or making a move, for example a change of direction, to beat his opponent. In the game, the Give and Go is usually used either between two guards or, more likely, between a guard and a forward. In this latter move the guard passes ahead to a forward and then cuts for basket for the return pass. If you are playing against an inexperienced defender and you pass ahead, as in a guard to forward move, the defender may be tempted to turn to see where the ball has gone; at this moment you are free and should immediately cut for basket, signalling for the return pass. Another opportunity to be prepared for is that your opponent may get off balance in an effort to intercept your pass. To make the immediate cut, you need to be well balanced, with knees flexed so you can make the quick start that will enable you to get past your opponent. Should your opponent not make an error, you can force one by using a change of direction and pace to beat

a

c

76   him (see fig. 63).

The Give and Go move aims to create a situation with two attacking players momentarily against one defender. An alternative method to beat an opponent is to use a roll to get free, as previously shown in fig. 8.

b

Fig. 63   Give and Go

d

Backdoor

Another method of beating an opponent when you do not have the ball, is to make use of a *backdoor* cut. This can be used when your opponent overplays the passing lane and prevents your team-mate passing you the ball. When this occurs, fake to move out to receive the ball, then reverse direction and move at speed towards the basket, signalling for the ball.

This move is not quite so simple as it may appear. Firstly, you are cutting to a position where there could be two defenders between yourself and the ball, and secondly, your team-mate holding the ball may not be alert to your move. When a Give and Go move is operated, the receiver should always watch to see what movement, if any, the person who passed the ball is making. With a backdoor

move the cutter is unlikely to have just passed and the operation of this move requires understanding and alertness (tell each other to look for this move). When looking for a team-mate to pass to, look ahead towards basket; your attention will then be in the right area of court to see his signal when he gets free.

Fig. 64   Backdoor

a

b

c

Fig. 65
Post play

Post Play

One of the basic screen situations that can be used in the game is a variation on the Give and Go. The attacker passes ahead and cuts to basket looking for the return pass, but instead of cutting and keeping space between himself and the ball handler as in the Give and Go, cuts close to his team-mate. This causes the marking defender to check his movement momentarily due to the position on court of the attacker's team-mate. This should then free the cutter for a return pass. This type of screen situation is called a *post play*.

In the post play illustrated in fig. 65, the pivot player has moved out from the under-basket area to receive a pass at the free throw line. Notice that he uses a jump stop in taking the ball and landing. The guard, after making the pass, cuts close to the pivot player, who pivots to turn his back on the opponent marking the guard. The guard is thus freed, and receives a pass and takes a shot before the defenders have had time to recover.

The basic post play action may be used from a number of different angles to the basket. A useful guide to its operation is that the player setting the post should attempt to take up a position along a straight line between the team-mate about to use the post and the basket. It does not have to be the pivot player who sets a post; it will frequently be a forward who creates a post for a team-mate to use.

In fig. 65 the player about to cut past the post after passing moves away from the direction of the cut, then changes direction and cuts past the post. This makes the task of the defending player more difficult. The player creating the post can pivot into the path of the defender, but the rules require that the opponent should be given a space of between one and two metres in which to stop and change direction. The attacking team expect that the defender will have his movements checked in this situation. The pivot by the player setting the post enables him to face the basket and this discourages the defender from switching to mark the cutting player.

In fig. 65 the player creating the post has moved out from the under-basket area to receive the pass. If you do this when setting a post, your team-mate will find it relatively easy to hit you with a pass and it will make it more difficult for your defender to interfere. The pass used will frequently be an overhead pass.

Pick Screen

The post play is not the only screen that players should be prepared to use and be able to recognise in the game. Remembering that the basic principle of the screen play is that an attacking player takes up a position that will prevent a defender reaching or maintaining a desired defensive position, two attacking players can co-operate to free one of the pair from his defender. In the post play, the cutter closes the gap between the team-mates, to create the screen situation. The screen situation can also be created by the player who is to set the screen converging on his team-mate, and stationing himself in such a position that when the team-mate moves the defender will find that he is unable to maintain his position due to the screen. This type of screen situation is usually referred to as a *pick screen*, and is illustrated in fig. 66 being used against a pressing defence in the mid-court area. The player with the ball, still having his dribble to come, is closely marked. His team-mate moves and takes up a position facing the ball handler's defender. The ball-handler then drives close to the screening player causing the defender to check his movement. When setting a pick screen, move in facing the opponent on whom you are to set the screen, endeavouring to land with a jump stop, taking a position with your two feet astride the line of the path that the defender will wish to take in following your team-mate. To be a legal screen you must be stationary when used by a team-mate; the advantage of setting the screen facing the opponent is that it enables you to see any movement that may be made by the defender and if necessary stop earlier than planned. Using a jump stop to set the screen is a clear signal to your team-mate that you have set the screen.

Fig. 66   Pick screen

b

c

Pick and Roll

The success of the screen may depend on a defender retaining his defensive responsibility to a particular attacking player. One method that defenders can use to oppose the opponents' efforts to use a screen situation is for the defender marking the player setting the screen to switch defensive responsibility onto the player who has moved free using the screen. The attacking team would still have a move they could use to counter this defence, however, and that would be for the screener to roll and move to basket. This particular move is illustrated in fig. 67, which

shows a forward setting a pick screen for a guard. The forward moves out from the base-line and sets the screen on the defender marking the guard. The guard uses this screen to drive for basket, and when the defender marking the forward steps out to deny the guard an unmarked drive for basket the forward pivots on his inside foot, turning so as to see the drive being made by his team-mate. This roll by the screener places the defensive player, who has been screened, at the back of the screener, thus creating a two versus one situation on the defender who has switched onto the

driver. The screener, having rolled, now signals and receives a pass as he moves free towards the basket. The fact that the rolling player should face the driver as he turns is important and can be applied to other situations in the game. In the illustration of the post play (fig. 65), notice that the post player, when he pivoted, faced the direction in which his team-mate moves. Similarly, on the Give and Go the forward, when he receives the pass from the guard, pivots to continue facing the movement of his team-mate. One time when you would turn your back on the team-mate who

a

b

has given you the ball is if you were
reversing on your opponent and
driving to basket to take advantage of
a mistake by your defender in
overplaying the pass.

Fig. 67   Pick and roll

c

d

Fig. 68   Screen off the ball

Screen Off the Ball

All the screen situations considered so far have involved the screen being set for a ball handler. Players should also be prepared to set, and make use of, a screen set off the ball. The post play covered earlier can be used with a third player holding the ball, the cutter losing his opponent on a post and when free receiving a pass from the ball handler. Fig. 68 shows a pick screen being set off the ball. The ball handler passes and instead of following his pass, he moves and sets the screen on a team-mate who does not have the ball. Once the screen is set this team-mate cuts towards the basket close to the screen and signals for the pass. When considering the backdoor move to get a player free, it was mentioned that a pass receiver should be aware of the movement being made by the team-mate who has given him the ball. This movement by the passer can alert the ball handler to the particular play being attempted by the team-mate. Thus he could be cutting for a return pass, as in a Give and Go; or cutting close to the ball handler as in a post play; or converging on the ball handler's defender, as in a pick screen; or, as in fig. 68, moving to set a screen off the ball.

Principles of Team Defence

It is possible to identify some basic ingredients of team defence which should form part of your understanding of the game as a player. It should be emphasised that players should be capable of applying the ideas that follow, and the fact that some ideas can be stated in few words, e.g. you should prevent passes into the danger area, does not mean that they are of little importance. Some very basic and very important defensive ideas can be stated briefly.

Aim

Your basic aim defensively is to obtain possession of the ball without allowing your opponents to score. The most common methods of gaining possession are by obtaining a rebound from a missed shot, or through a violation of the rules by your opponents, or through a passing error by the attacking team. You may be able to force the passing error by pressuring the passer or by marking passing lanes; but you will find it more difficult to force your opponents to break the rules. Your pressure on passes may lead to the ball being thrown out of court. By the use of good defensive footwork to maintain a position between the dribbler and basket you may force him to commit a

charging foul or to travel when he attempts to stop quickly. By working hard as a team unit it may be possible to discourage your opponents from shooting for a long time and so force them to break the 30-second rule. The most important method you will use to obtain possession is the taking of a rebound from a missed shot. Which shots are liable to miss? Basically the low percentage shots, which are the long range shots and the forced shots against close-marking defenders. An important ingredient of good team defence therefore is the defending of the high percentage scoring area.

Defending the High Percentage Scoring Area

This we can consider under two headings, defending the ball and defending against a man.
When **defending the ball**, a player will endeavour to prevent shots in the high percentage scoring area, and drives and passes into this area.
When **defending against an opponent**, a player will endeavour to prevent him receiving the ball in the danger area by overplaying passing lanes, prevent him gaining a rebound by blocking out, and prevent him gaining a position advantage.

Matching Attacking Patterns

One theme that has been repeated on a number of occasions in this book concerns the use of space. The attacking team will endeavour to dictate where space occurs, through the formation they use. Defenders should match their pattern and defend space in the high percentage scoring area that the attacking team want to leave clear. This is done by using a sagging man-to-man or a zone defence. These give the vital depth to the defence.

Pressure to the Ball

Defence should not be thought of as completely negative, with the defensive team waiting for the attacking team to move. Defenders can take the initiative by trying to pressure their opponents into errors. This can be done by playing defence over the whole court either from a man-to-man formation or using a zone. In these pressure defences, players will mark the ball and the close range passing lanes from the ball handler, leaving available only long range passes that defenders will have time to cover. This pressure to the ball could occur in a non-pressing defence, in that passes into the high percentage scoring area can be marked and discouraged.

Organisation

Your coach will specify the defensive tactic you will employ and his instructions could include, for example, use of a particular zone formation or use of a particular tactic such as sliding to combat screen plays.

Communication

The defensive team should talk to each other, so that all members of the team are aware of attacking moves and defensive commitments. When using a zone defence the ball handler should be marked by one defender, and this defender should tell teammates that he is responsible for marking the ball. This enables teammates to organise their defensive play in relation to the ball.

Importance of Individual Defence

Finally, but most important, good team defence depends upon good individual defence.

Defending Against the Basic Two-versus-Two Attacking Plays

Defence against the basic two-versus-two attacking plays that were covered earlier in this book will depend upon good individual defence and the application of simple tactics. A number of these attacking moves involved the attacking player passing and then moving free; for you as a defender the situation when your opponent has just passed the ball is a potentially dangerous one to which

you must be alert. When the man you are marking passes, keep alert. If you have been marking a player who was a shooting threat you will have been close to him; without the ball he is no longer a scoring threat and you should sag.

Fig. 69 shows the defender sagging after the man he is marking passes the ball. Notice that the defender not only sags but also changes his stance so he can see the ball and the man he is marking. To have kept his right foot forward would have placed the defender at a disadvantage, so he drops this foot back as he takes up his new stance. Note how he keeps his arms up with one arm towards his opponent and the other to the ball. The footwork is the same that you would

a   Fig. 69   Defender sagging when his opponent passes   b

Fig. 70   *Defensive player sliding to combat a screen play*

a

use if you were marking with right foot
forward and your opponent started to
dribble to your right; your first move in
this situation would be to drop your
right foot back.

If you are playing well as a defender
you will find that every time the attacking team moves the ball you will
move or change your defensive
position.

When defending against a team
using screens, it is vital that the
defender whom your opponents are
attempting to screen knows that the
screen is there. Talking between
team-mates must occur. If you realise
that the opponent you are marking
has created a screen situation you
must alert your team-mate to this. He
will thus know the screen is there and

b

c

c

Zone Defence

should use one hand to feel where it is stationed. He will then try to go 'over the top' of the screen, which means he moves keeping between his opponent and the screen. Should this fail then he can use the move shown in fig. 70, i.e. sliding. In this the defender marking the player using the screen (white no. 5) moves behind the screener as he follows his opponent. Notice that his defensive team-mate assists him in sliding by stepping back and guiding him through. The disadvantage with sliding is that the attacking player no. 5 could make a quick stop and shoot, using his team-mate as a front screen.

An alternative defence to the screen is for the defenders to switch defensive responsibility. It has been seen that the attacking team will combat this with the screener rolling for basket. Use of the switch demands good team-work and understanding between defenders if it is to operate successfully.

Remember that if an opponent sets a screen on you, and the opponent you are marking is outside his shooting range, the simplest way to combat the screen is to sag. This will give you more time in which to avoid the

screen. Screen plays should only be successful against close-marking defenders, which means that the screen off the ball should not work, as you will sag away from a player who does not have the ball!

One defensive tactic that a coach may employ is for a team to use a zone defence. Two commonly-used starting zone formations are the 2.1.2 and the 1.3.1 patterns, as illustrated in figs. 71 and 72.

The way in which a coach makes his team work as a unit from these patterns can vary. In our opinion the following points should be noted when a zone defence is being used: you should mark the ball handler as though you were marking him man-to-man; the next potential receivers of the ball should also be marked man-to-man; the zone should create depth so that the man marking the ball is covered by another defensive team-mate; players in the zone should keep their hands up to force passes to the 'free' attacking players to go round the outside of the zone. A zone depends for its success on a team's ability to work as a team unit, and for this to occur communication is essential. Fig. 73 shows a 2.1.2 zone defending against the ball being held by an opposing forward in the corner. Note how all the defensive players have moved to the ball and that potential pass receivers are marked.

Fig. 71   2.1.2 zone pattern

Fig. 72   1.3.1 zone pattern

Fig. 73   2.1.2 zone marking the ball in the corner

Fig. 74   1.3.1 attacking formation against a
          2.1.2 zone defence to create a medium range
          shot

Fig. 75   Shooting over a front screen against
          a zone defence

Attacking Play against Zone Defences

Each defender in a zone defence is responsible for a particular zone in the formation, and as the defence will not be complete as a unit until all five defenders are in position, the first attacking weapon to use is the fast break. Only when the fast break is unsuccessful should other weaknesses of a zone defence be attacked.

To attack these weaknesses you will frequently need patience to create an opening, so a change of tempo should occur in your play if the fast break does not lead to a score.

With each defender responsible for a zone, there will be points in the defence where the zones of responsibility of two defenders meet. This is a point of weakness in the zone defence, so obviously this is a position at which to station attacking players. Another weakness of a zone is that they defend to the ball and can be out-manoeuvred by rapid passing. Fig. 74 shows a 1.3.1 attacking formation being used against a 2.1.2 zone defence. This stations attacking players in the 'gaps' between defenders. As the defender moves to mark the ball, a quick pass to the left forward leaves the latter with space for a shot.

Most teams employ a zone defence to cover the high percentage scoring area under the basket. An obvious method of beating them is to increase the area of court that is a high percentage scoring area for your team, thus shooting and scoring over the top of the zone. To give yourself more space for the shot you should use a different attacking formation to the pattern of the zone defence. To give more time for a shot over the zone a front screen can also be used. Fig. 75 shows a forward in the corner shooting over a front screen against a 2.1.2 zone defence. You will frequently find that the zone defenders allow a player in the corner of the court to move closer to basket for his shot than they would an attacking player at the front. This attacking move against a zone defence creates an 'overload' against the one defender who has two attacking players within his zone. When an attacker starts scoring from outside the zone, the defence should move out to mark him, thus leaving more space closer to basket.

Fast Break

Fig. 76   Fast break—outlet pass after opponents score

Possession of the ball is the difference between being on attack and being on defence. At the time of the change from one state to the other, the team that has gained possession should, if they can attack immediately, have their opponents at a disadvantage. This is the fast break and is the first attacking play that every team should use. The aim is to take the ball down court into a scoring position in the front court before the opponents have had time to cover and to organise their defence. If your team is to make use of the fast break you as a player will need to keep alert to the change of possession so that you may respond quickly.

We will consider the fast break in three phases: the outlet pass to get the break started; the effort to fill three lanes as you take the ball down court; and the final phase where your team aims to take the first good shot created.

Outlet Pass

At this point in the break, the reaction of the team to the change of possession is vital. Figs. 76 and 77 show two situations, one after a score by the opponents and the other after the

94

team about to break has gained the rebound.

After the score, the player nearest the ball as it scores should quickly take the ball one step off court (one foot is sufficient if the other is lifted) and immediately pass the ball in court. In fig. 76 the player making the outlet pass from out of bounds throws the ball, using a one-hand pass, in to a team-mate who has broken out to the side. The player taking the ball out must operate at speed, for the time that he takes in stepping off court and throwing the ball in will give the opponents time to move back on defence and prevent the 'new' attacking team gaining a numerical advantage at the end of their break.

Outlet Pass from a Rebound

Upon gathering a defensive rebound the 'new' attacking team should aim to pass the ball from the congested under-basket area as quickly as possible. In fig. 77 the tall pivot player of the defensive team is seen gathering the rebound while a team-mate breaks to a position at the side (about level with the free throw lane) where he receives the outlet pass from the pivot player. The outlet pass

to the side has the advantage of clearing the middle of the court, which could well be congested. After gathering a rebound a player may find that he has space to dribble

off straight down court, and he should do this if he does not have a team-mate free ahead of the ball.

Fig. 77 Outlet pass from a rebound

a

b

Filling the Lanes

This should occur as the ball is brought down court following the outlet pass of the ball from the under-basket area. Obviously, if the opponents are very slow moving back to defence on the loss of possession, the player who receives the outlet pass may be able to drive all the way down court for an uncontested shot. Even if this does occur, his team-mates should not just stand back and watch—he may miss the shot. A team will only be able to fast break successfully if all its members strive to be in on the break, aiming to move quickly down court so that the team has a chance to outnumber the opponents at the end of the break. As a team breaks down court, the players aim to fill three lanes, one player going down the middle and the other two down each side. Fig. 78 shows an attacking player dribbling the ball on a fast break down the middle of court; his team-mates have joined him and filled the two outside lanes, thus creating space between offensive players, a basic principle of team offence. Bringing the ball down court, the attacking team may either inter-pass the ball or leave one player to dribble it. Having established a position in one of the lanes in the fast break, a player should endeavour to retain his position in that lane; players will fill lanes in relation to other members of the team, and constant lane-switching will confuse team-mates.

Final Phase of the Fast Break

As the team bring the ball into the scoring area, they should endeavour to have the ball with the player who is in the middle lane. If he can, this player should try to go all the way to basket and only pass off when his forward progress is blocked. If the ball is in the middle this player has the option of passing to either side. Fig. 79 shows the ball with the middle player who has come to a halt as a defender moves in to stop him at the top of the free throw lane. Notice the team-mates who have filled the outside lanes continuing their run down court; as they reach an area near the head of the free throw lane they should cut in towards the basket, signalling for a pass.

79

80

Defence Against a Fast Break

To stop opponents gaining a numerical advantage through the use of a fast break, the defensive team should aim to delay the break starting, defensively fast break and, if the opponents do succeed in gaining a numerical advantage, try to delay their shot.

To delay the start of the break the attacking rebounder should endeavour to mark the opposing player who has rebounded, and stop him making a quick outlet pass—see fig. 81. Notice that the team trying to stop the fast break have moved a player out to mark the opposing player who has moved out to the side to receive the outlet pass.

Should your opponents succeed in gaining a numerical advantage, you should mark the under-basket area and force them to take the long shot or to make additional passes that will give your team-mates time to recover.

Fig. 80 Fast Break. The defensive team have used a defensive fast break to prevent their opponents gaining a numerical advantage, and the attacking player with the ball (who has his defender at a disadvantage, with his legs crossed) prepares to take the first good shot offered. Attacking team-mates are running to ensure they are in on the break and available to rebound should the shot miss

98

Fig. 81 *Defending against a fast break by delaying the outlet pass*

81

In fig. 82 a situation is shown in which three attacking players are attacking two defenders. The two defenders set up in a tandem formation, one under the basket and the other in front. The player at the front of the tandem aims to stop the ball, thus forcing a pass to the side. As the ball goes to the side the defender under the basket moves out to mark the ball handler, and the player who was at the front of the tandem moves back to cover the under-basket area and to stop the pass across to the player on the opposite side. The defenders are thus defending from the basket out: prevent the lay up shot, even if it gives a jump shot; defend the jump shot even if it gives a set shot from a long range.

82a

Fig. 82 *Defending against a fast break, using a tandem formation when playing two against three*

82b

99

Fig. 83   *Demonstration jump ball at the centre circle*

Special Situations

During the game there are a number of special situations occurring to which players must be alert. These are jump balls, free throws and out-of-bounds situations. Your coach may wish you to use some specific tactics in these situations, so we will cover some general points which need your attention as a player.

Jump Ball

A demonstration jump ball at the centre is shown in fig. 83; notice that players are marking opponents (between opponent and basket) round the circle. Using this formation both jumpers have a position to tip the ball to the safe tipping zone, where two team-mates stand side by side. The jumper may wish to tip the ball forward as shown. Note that the player about to catch the ball has moved into the circle—as soon as the ball is touched by one of the jumpers you may cross the line of the circle. Prior to the tip, players should concentrate on the jumpers, being particularly alert to the hands of the jumpers on the ball.

100

Fig. 84   Jump ball at free throw line

In the jump ball at free throw line illustrated in fig. 84, notice that the defensive team have gained the position on the circle closest to their basket. When a jump ball is called at a free throw line, both teams should move quickly to gain this position. An attacking pivot player in this position is a considerable threat, for should he catch the ball, he can step to either left or right and be very close to basket. In fig. 84, the white team did not anticipate gaining the tip and have therefore taken up a defensive position with no. 6 back prepared for the fast break.

Free Throw

Fig. 85, a demonstration free throw, shows how the players who have lined up are ready to move in; note their bent knees. We would expect white player no. 15 to step across in front of his opponent to block him out. The white team have one player (no. 8) lined up ready to move into the lane to block out the shooter. They have also stationed a player (no. 10) at the side ready to receive an outlet pass.

Out of Bounds

In the section on fast break, it was mentioned that following a basket, a player should quickly take the ball out of bounds for a fast throw-in. It would be dangerous, however, to use this on every throw-in; there are five seconds in which to release the ball and you should be prepared to use them. Players must be alert to move free to receive the in-bounds pass. Remember that defensively you have five players on court to your opponents' four and as fig. 86 shows, the 'spare' defender can be used to prevent a pass in from out-of-bounds to a tall opposing pivot player.

Fig. 85   Demonstration free throw

Fig. 86   Defensive team sagging onto the pivot player in an out-of-bounds situation

Training

The organisation of team training sessions will be an important part of the duties of your club coach. During training sessions he will organise practices (called 'Drills' in basketball) to enable you to learn the techniques we have covered in this book, and to improve the level of your skill through repetitive practice in a variety of situations. As detailed information on training sessions is more appropriate to a book for teachers and coaches, training coverage here is limited to advice to players working outside organised club sessions. The coverage can be divided into two headings: (i) technique and skill; and (ii) conditioning.

Technique and Skill

The need for players to practise their shooting should be stressed. It has already been suggested that it is a good idea to fix a basketball ring in your back garden, so you can spend some spare moments shooting. If you aim to reach the top in the game you should endeavour to take 250–300 shots on most days of the week. If you have a chance to work in a gymnasium with a partner you could use the practice illustrated in fig. 87. One player stands under the basket,

collecting rebounds and feeding the shooter who takes a set number of shots (e.g. 10, 20, or 25) before they change round. This shot could be taken from the spot where the ball is received, following a quick stop after a cut to receive the ball; or following a short dribble. An alternative practice to do with a partner is for one player to shoot while the other defends, to make the shooting situation more realistic. If you are alone on the court you should vary your practice, taking shots from different spots on the floor; aim to score ten baskets from one spot before you move to the next.

Fig. 87   Shooting practice in pairs

Fig. 88   *Two-versus-two and one-versus-one practices*

Fig. 89   *Defensive footwork practice*

Conditioning

Conditioning for sport is a vast topic and a number of books have been written on the subject, for example *Conditioning for Sport* by Dr. Nick Whitehead in the EP Sport series. The game of basketball involves non-stop action and if players are to succeed they will need to be in good physical condition, capable of sustained work over a long period. Coaches should make organised training sessions hard work, and should keep players active. The hardest physical work is in defence, where players are expected to maintain their defensive stance, with knees bent, and move using this stance constantly. A good practice that coaches could use is shown in fig. 89. The players stand in front of the coach, who directs them to move in one direction and then another. Throughout this movement the players aim to retain their defensive stance and to use a shuffle step to move. You may undertake a similar exercise working alone, taking up the defensive stance and then moving forwards, backwards, to the side and diagonally. If you move 6 to 10 feet in each direction and then return to your starting position this will prevent you favouring movement in one direction during your practice.

88

Two other useful practices you can use inside if there are other players available are to play games of one-versus-one or two-versus-two. These are half-court games in which the 'team' (one or two players) aims to score into one basket against the other 'team'. On the loss of possession the opponent(s) take the ball to the half-way line and attack the same basket. Alternatively the 'team' attacks for a set number of times, counting the baskets scored before changing over. Both these practices enable you to practise a number of the skills of the game in a competitive situation. Fig.

88 shows both these games being played into the same basket, with the two-versus-two game being played on the left-hand side of the court. In the two-versus-two game you can see the attacking team using a screen, with the defensive player marking the player with the ball trying to avoid the screen by going over the top of it so as to retain his defensive position. In the one-versus-one game the attacking player has dribbled in to the under-basket area and is trying to create space for the shot.

Sustained running is one way to improve your ability to withstand the physical demands of the game, and can be particularly beneficial at the beginning of the season. Find a course of about three miles' length and run this at least three times a week. The game requires quick bursts of speed over the relatively short distance of the court and shuttle runs should therefore also be included in your training. Fig. 90 shows a team training using shuttle runs. They are making use of the standard markings on the court to measure out their shuttles. They start and finish each shuttle at the end line; the first run is to touch the free throw line and back to the end line, next to the centre line, then to the far free throw line and finally to the far end line and back to the starting end line to finish. Using this routine you should sprint at top speed on each shuttle, touching each line with your hands as you turn. Aim to do at least three shuttle runs during each training session. The shuttles could be undertaken dribbling the ball if you want a variation on this routine, but this will be less strenuous.

During the game you will need to jump to shoot, to rebound and at jump balls. It is not always the tallest player who wins out at these situations, but rather the player who jumps the highest. A part of your training should include some work on your jumping. A good routine to use is touching the backboard. Start by standing directly under the backboard, and jump as high as possible to touch the board, continuing to jump with no stop between the jumps for at least 30 seconds. This practice can be varied to working with a ball; start under the basket, jump and shoot up one side of the basket, gather the rebound and jump and shoot up the other side. Continue this for at least 30 seconds.

Fig. 91   Touching backboard training routine

Glossary of Basketball Terms

Originally published in the English Basket Ball Association's Coaching Booklet *A Guide for the Potential Basketball Coach* and reproduced by permission.

Basketball, like other sports, has its own 'jargon' used to describe certain aspects of playing the game. Often a number of different names are given to the same action and, of course, many terms have their origin in the rules of the game. Most of the terms originating from the rules have been omitted and where they are given, the fact that the term comes from the rules has been noted. Where more than one term is used the most popular one has been defined. It is hoped that through the use of a standard terminology, communication and understanding will be improved between coaches, players and officials.

Alive—offensive player who has the ball, but has not dribbled.

Assist—a pass to an open teammate that results in an immediate score.

Back Court—that half of the court which contains a team's defensive basket.

Backdoor—a term used to describe a cut by an offensive player towards the basket to the side of the defensive player away from the ball. It is mainly used when the offensive player is being overplayed or when the defence turns to look at the ball or in another direction.

Ball Control Game—a type of offensive play that emphasises maintaining possession of the ball until a good shot is possible.

Baseline Drive—a drive (q.v.) made close to the offensive end line of the court.

Blocking—'Is personal contact which impedes the progress of an opponent who is not in possession of the ball.' (Rules)

Blocking Out (Blocking off) (Boxing out) (Cutting out)—the positioning of the defensive player in such a manner as to prevent an offensive player from moving to the basket to gain a rebound.

Break—the rapid movement of a player to a space where he hopes to receive a pass.

Brush-Off (Brush-off screen)—to cause one's opponent to run into a third player thus 'losing' him momentarily.

Buttonhook—to move in one direction, turn sharply and double back.

Centre—the name of one of the positions on the team, usually the tallest player in the team. The pivot player (q.v.).

Charging—a personal foul caused by a player making bodily contact by running into an opponent. Usually committed by an offensive player.

Chaser—a defender whose duty is to harass the offensive players, usually the front man or men in a zone defence (q.v.).

Circulation—a player's movements about the court on offence.

Clear Out—an offensive manoeuvre in which players vacate an area of court so as to isolate one offensive player and one defensive player. This offensive player may then attempt to score against his opponent who has

Fig. 92   Blocking out

no defensive team-mates close enough to help him.

Combination Defence—a team defence where some of the team play zone defence (q.v.) and others man-to-man defence (q.v.).

Control Basketball (Possession Basketball)—a style of play in which a team deliberately makes sure of every pass and only shoots when there is a very high percentage chance of scoring.

Controlling the Boards—gaining the majority of the rebounds.

Cut—a quick movement by an offensive player without the ball to gain an advantage over the defence, usually directed towards the basket.

Cutter—a player who cuts (q.v.) or breaks (q.v.).

Cutaway—a player's move in cutting for basket after setting up a screen (q.v.) situation.

Dead—an offensive player who has used his dribble.

Double Team—when two defensive players mark one opponent with the ball, usually a temporary measure. See Trap.

Drill—a repetitive practice designed to improve one or more particular fundamental skills or team combinations.

Drive—the movement of an offensive player while aggressively dribbling towards the basket in an attempt to score.

Dunk—a shot in which a jumping player puts the ball down into the opponent's basket from above.

Fake (Feint)—a movement made with the aim of deceiving an opponent.

Fall-Away—a method of performing certain shots and passes in which the

Fig. 93   Brush-off

Fig. 94 Drive

Fig. 95 Fake shot

player with the ball moves in one direction as the ball moves in another.

Fast Break (Quick Break)—a fast offence that attempts to advance the ball to the front court before the defence is organised, with the object of achieving numerical superiority to give a good shot.

Feed—to pass the ball to a team-mate who is in a scoring position.

Feint—see Fake.

Floating—a manoeuvre in man-to-man defence where a defender marking an opponent on the weak side (q.v.) stays between his opponent and the basket, but because the ball is on the opposite side of the court, moves laterally towards it.

Floor Play—used to describe the movements on the court of players of either team.

Forward—the name of one of the positions in the team. The forwards play on offence in the area of court, either on the right- or left-hand side, between the restricted area (q.v.) and the side lines.

Fouled Out—being required to leave the game after committing five fouls.

Foul Line—free throw line.

Free Ball (Loose Ball)—a ball which although in play is not in the possession of either team.

Freelance—an unstructured type of offence where players take advantage of whatever offensive opportunities arise.

Freezing the Ball (Stall)—the action of a team in possession of the ball who attempt to retain possession of the ball without an attempt to score. Limited to 30 seconds and often used late in the game in an effort to protect a slight lead.

Front Court—that half of the court which contains the basket which a team is attacking.

Front Screen—a screen set up by an offensive player between a team-mate and this team-mate's opponent.

Fronting the Pivot—guarding the pivot player (q.v.) in front rather than between him and the basket. A defensive tactic aiming to prevent a good pivot player from receiving the ball close to the basket.

Full-Court Press—a pressing defence which operates throughout the whole court and not merely in the defender's back court (q.v.). See Press.

Fig. 96   Jump ball

Fundamentals—the basic skills of the game, necessary as a background for all team play.

Give and Go—an offensive manoeuvre in which a player passes the ball to a team-mate and cuts (q.v.) towards basket for a return pass.

Guard (Playmaker) (Quarterback)—the name of one of the positions on the team, usually played by the shorter players, who on offence will play in the area of court between the centre line and the free throw line extended to the side-lines.

Half-Court Press—a pressing defence which operates in a team's back court.

Held Ball—'is declared when two players of opposing teams have one or both hands firmly on the ball, or held ball may be called when one closely guarded player does not pass, shoot, bat, roll or dribble the ball within 5 seconds'. (Rules)

High—a position played by an offen-

Fig. 97   Lead pass

sive player who plays in the area of court away from the end line near to the free throw line.

In-Line—the basic man-to-man defensive position 'in line' between the opponent and the basket being defended.

Inside— (i) in the under-basket area.
(ii) between the perimeter of the defence and the basket they are defending.
(iii) 'inside' the key (q.v.).

Jump Ball—'a jump ball takes place when the official tosses the ball between two opposing players . (Rules)

Key (Keyhole)—the restricted area (q.v.) including the circle, derived from the original keyhole shape.

Lane—see Restricted Area.

Lead Pass—a pass thrown ahead of the intended receiver so that he can catch the ball on the move and maintain his speed.

Low—a position held by an offensive player operating in the area of court near to the end line or basket.

Man-to-Man Defence—a style of defence where each player is assigned to guard a specific opponent regardless of where he goes in his offensive manoeuvres.

Off-Line—a variation of 'in-line' defence (q.v.), in which the defender takes up a position slightly to one side of his opponent but still between the opponent and the basket. The aim is to reduce the opponent's offensive options.

One-to-One (1 v. 1)—the situation where one offensive player attacks one defensive player.

Options—alternative offensive manoeuvres that can occur in a game situation.

Out-of-Bounds—the area outside the legal playing court, i.e. outside the inside edge of the lines marking the side-lines and the end-lines.

Outlet Pass—the first pass made after a defensive rebound (q.v.), usually made to a player stationed near to the closest sideline of the court and used to initiate a fast break (q.v.).

Outside— (i) nearer the sideline of the court.
(ii) between the sideline and the perimeter of

Fig. 98   Man-to-man defence

Fig. 99   Outlet pass

the defence.

(iii) 'outside' the key (q.v.).

Overload—outnumber.

Overtime—the extra period(s) played after the expiration of the second half of a game in which the score has been tied. Play is continued for an extra period of 5 minutes or as many such periods of 5 minutes as may be necessary to break the tie.

Pass and Cut—see Give and Go.

Pattern—the predetermined positional formation adopted by an offensive team prior to their initiating offensive manoeuvres. Common patterns are 1.3.1 and 2.3.

Pattern Play—offensive plays initiated from fixed and pre-determined court positions.

Pick (Side-screen)—a screen (q.v.) set at the side of a team-mate's opponent.

Pick and Roll—a side screen followed by a pivot towards the basket by the player who has set the screen, useful against a switching man-to-man defence.

Pivot Player—usually the tallest player in the team who operates on offence in an area near the sides of, and occasionally in, the free throw lane and close to the basket. He is stationed there for scoring purposes and to feed cutters (q.v.) and is a player around whom the offensive team pivot. He is sometimes called a post player.

Post— (i) see Pivot Player.

(ii) an offensive manoeuvre in which a player takes up a position, usually with his back to the basket he is attacking, thus providing a target to receive a pass and/or act as a rear screen (q.v.) to enable team-mates to run their opponents into the post.

Press—a defensive attempt to force the opposing team into making some kind of error and thus lose possession of the ball. It is accomplished usually by aggressive defence, double teaming (q.v.) or harassing the ball handler with attempts to tie-up (q.v.) the ball. The press can be applied full court, half court or any other fractional part of the playing area and can be based on either man-to-man or zone (q.v.) principles.

Quarterback—see guard. A term derived from American Football.

Quick Break—see Fast Break.

Rebound—a term used to describe the actual retrieving of the ball as it rebounds from the backboard or the ring after an unsuccessful shot (see fig. 100).

OFFENSIVE REBOUND— therefore means gaining the rebound from the team's offensive basket (i.e. the one it is attacking).

DEFENSIVE REBOUND— is retrieving the ball from the team's defensive basket (i.e. the basket it is defending).

Rebound Triangle—a term used to describe the positioning of a group of three defenders who form a triangle around the basket after a shot has been attempted. The aim is to cover the probable positions of the ball should a rebound occur and prevent an opponent from gaining a good position from which to collect the rebound.

Restraining Circles—the circles 3·60 metres (12 feet) in diameter located in the centre of the court and at the free throw lines.

Fig. 100   Rebounding

Restricted Areas—'The restricted areas shall be spaces marked in the court which are limited by the end lines, the free throw lines and by lines which originate at the end lines, their outer edges being 3 metres from the midpoints of the end lines, and terminate at the end of the free throw lines.' (Rules)

Reverse (Roll)—a change of direction in which the offensive player endeavours to free himself from a close-marking defender. The change of direction is executed after a move towards the defender and a pivot so that the offensive player turns his back on his opponent and then moves off in the new direction.

Safety Man—an offensive player who plays in the guard position with the aim of defending against possible fast breaks on loss of possession and to receive a pass when an offensive play breaks down.

Sag—when a defender moves away from his opponent towards the basket he is defending.

Sagging Defence—a team defensive tactic in which the defenders farthest from the ball sag away from their opponents towards the basket to help their team-mates and cover the high percentage scoring area.

Screen—a screen occurs when an offensive player attempts to prevent a defender from reaching a desired position or maintaining his defensive position. The screen is intended to impede the progress of the defender so that the offensive player he is marking has an unimpeded shot or a clear path to basket.

Scrimmage—a practice game.

Set Play— (i) a repetitive, prearranged form of offence.
(ii) a play executed to predetermined and rehearsed moves which, when applied at certain set situations in the game, are intended to result in a favourable scoring chance. The set situations are usually out-of-bounds, jump-ball or the free-throw situation.

Set Up—the action of establishing an offensive pattern (q.v.) or the defensive organisation.

Series—a name given to a number of plays used by an offensive team in particular situations, e.g. High Post Plays.

Slow Break—a deliberate attack against a defence that is set up (q.v.).

Slide—when a defensive player, in order to prevent himself being screened, moves, as he follows his own opponent, between a team-mate and that team-mate's opponent.

Stall—see Freezing the Ball.

Steal—to take the ball away from an opponent.

Strong Side—refers to the side of the court on which the offensive team has the ball (at any one time).

Switch—a defensive manoeuvre in which two defenders exchange defensive responsibilities by changing the men they are guarding. It occurs usually during a screen situation in which one of the defenders can no longer guard his man because of the screen.

System—a team's basic offensive and defensive plays.

Tie-Up—a defensive situation in which the defenders through their defensive tactics gain a held ball (q.v.) situation.

Tip—the momentary catching and pushing of the ball towards the basket, executed by an offensive rebounder in an attempt to score from an offensive rebound (q.v.) while he is still in the air.

Tip-Off—the centre jump-ball at the start of play.

Trailer—an offensive player who follows behind the ball-handler.

Trap—a 'double team' (q.v.) in which two defenders attempt to stop a dribbler and prevent him from making a successful pass.

Transposition—occurs after the change of possession as a team moves from offence to defence and vice versa.

Turnover—the loss of ball possession without there having been an attempt by the offensive team to shoot at basket.

Weak Side—the opposite side of the court to the strong side (q.v.), that is, away from the ball.

Zone Defence—a team's defensive tactic in which the five defensive players react to the ball and in so doing are each responsible for an area of the court in which they move in relation to the movements of the ball.

Fig. 101   *The E.B.B.A. National Junior Championship Final, 1975*